NORTON DOMINATOR TWINS

1949 - 1970

Roy Bacon

First published in the United Kingdom by:
Niton Publishing
PO Box 3. Ventnor. Isle of Wight PO38 2AS

Acknowledgements
The author would like to thank those who helped this book by supplying the photographs. Most came from the EMAP archives or *Motor Cycle News* by courtesy of the editor, Malcolm Gough. Others came from the Mick Woollet archive and some from the author's files.

This edition published 1995 by
The Promotional Reprint Company Ltd,
exclusively for Selecta Book Limited,
Roundway, Devizes, Wiltshire SN10 2HR
and Reed Editions in Australia.

ISBN 1 85648 306 1

Printed in Hong Kong

A 1962 650 out on test and hauling a sidecar along, something at first thought impossible with the Featherbed frame.

Contents

Introduction

For the years between the wars, and for some time after the second, Norton were considered to be a firm who built, and raced, motorcycles with single-cylinder engines. They were also looked upon as a firm of honest, upright character, rather like their vertical-cylinder singles, an inheritance from the founder, James Norton.

In fact, while he did lay that foundation, and the singles always had upright cylinders, the early Nortons of the Edwardian era were twins. It was one such machine that won the first TT in 1907, but soon after that, the firm turned to singles and stayed with them until late in 1948. Then they announced a new vertical twin for, like the rest of the industry, they had to have one to sell against the highly successful Triumph model, which had stolen a huge lead after its introduction late in 1937.

All the major British firms brought out vertical twins in the early post-war era, but Norton finished up with two aces. The first was as a result of their engine being basically a sound design with an excellent combustion chamber, so it was to continue in production for nearly 30 years. The other was the renowned Featherbed frame, which set the standard against which the rest were measured. It did not come in with the first twin, but the twin was the first road model to use it, and it served for nearly two decades.

In time, the twin engine was made larger, and off-road and sidecar variants were built. Then came a degree of rear enclosure and, after that, the very sporting SS models. There were further capacity increases for the late 1960s and, later in that decade, some group variations using AJS and Matchless parts.

Before the end of the decade, the old style was replaced by the new Commando (covered in another in this series), but the Featherbed model did reach 1970 before it was finally dropped. Its frame, forks and wheels often lived on, or found a new lease of life as a Triton. For many riders, the latter was the best of both worlds - the easily-tuned Triumph engine in the Norton frame with its fine handling.

Dick Clayton on his 1951 ISDT Dominator where he used the Manx frame, twin engine and conical front hub - the machine the forerunner of the Model 88.

Model 7

The Norton twin first appeared as the Dominator Model 7 at the Earls Court Show held in November 1948. Its cycle parts were based on the single-cylinder ES2 model, and it had a modified form of the Norton gearbox and a brand new engine, designed by Bert Hopwood. Previously, he had worked on the Ariel Square Four and Triumph twin, so was no stranger to multi-cylinder engines. Later, he was to go on to BSA to design their A10.

In fact, the Hopwood engine was not Norton's first attempt at a vertical twin, for Jack Moore had designed one just after the war. This was on the lines of the Triumph with two camshafts and separate, light-alloy rocker boxes. Unlike the Triumph, however, access for valve adjustment was via side plates, each of which was held in place by a single knurled-head screw.

Photographs of the factory mock-up showed the stock ES2 cycle parts

The first Model 7 Dominator twin of 1949 with its revised gearbox but otherwise using the single cylinder cycle parts, including the plunger frame.

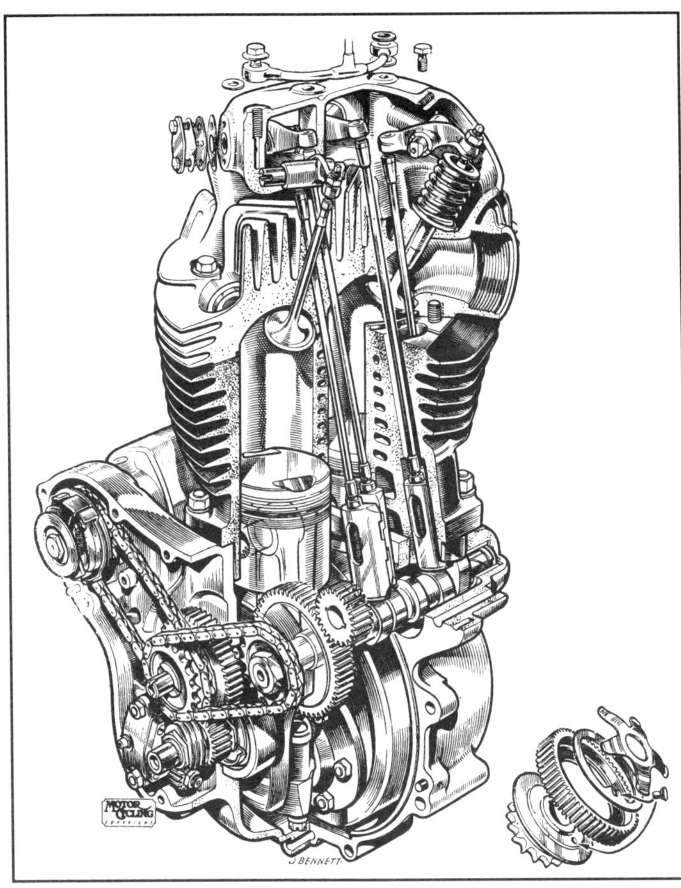

Cutaway drawing of the Norton twin engine which remained unchanged in its basics for three decades. This is the 596 cc version and it still retains the original dynamo drive.

in the plunger frame, but the model was never built. Hopwood joined Norton early in 1947, and his design was to reflect his opinion of the Triumph twin's weak points and, no doubt, a wish to produce something that was noticeably different. In this, he succeeded.

The new Norton engine was in the pattern of other British vertical twins which, invariably, had a 360-degree crankshaft, as this gave an even exhaust note and suited the fitment of a single carburettor and standard twin-cylinder magneto. It did nothing to overcome the inherent lack of balance of the engine, which was similar to that of a single, but this was not really a problem at the engine speeds of the time. Later, as engines grew in size, produced more power, and ran at higher speeds, it was to become significant and, for Norton, eventually led to the Commando model with its unique Isolastic engine mounting system.

This was still some two decades in the future, however, and the twin

The rigid frame version of the Dominator which was proposed for sidecar drivers but never offered for sale.

unveiled for 1949 had the engine mounted so that its cylinders were vertical. The gearbox was a separate unit, but tucked in well, and the cycle parts featured the Roadholder telescopic front forks and plunger rear suspension of the singles.

The overhead valve, twin cylinder engine had dimensions of 66 x 72.6 mm, which gave it a capacity of 497 cc. It was constructed in a manner that was conventional for the period, except that both gears and chains were used in the camshaft drive. The cylinder head and block were both one-piece iron castings, and although the 1949 brochure indicated that light-alloy components were available at an extra charge, these did not materialise. A light-alloy cylinder head did appear in time, but not the block, which remained in cast-iron for all production models. The engine lubrication was on the dry-sump system and the electrics employed the Lucas magneto and dynamo that were common at the time.

The light-alloy crankcase castings had a vertical joint on the centre-line of the engine with a single main bearing for the crankshaft in each. Both were of the same physical size, but that on the drive-side was a roller race, while the timing-side main was a ball race. An oil seal went outboard of the roller race, and an oil sealing disc beside the timing-side bearing.

Each crankcase half had a bridge cast across its mouth, adjacent to the split line, to stabilise the casting at the important joint between the top and bottom halves. The two castings were spigoted at their joint, with two locating dowels to assist, and were clamped together by a ring of fasteners.

The right-hand, or timing-side, casting included the timing chest, which was extended fore and aft for the drives to the electrical accessories. The chest also extended down to include the oil pump, and a single timing cover enclosed all the drives and parts. Both crankcase castings had a small sump formed in them to enable the oil to collect before being returned to the external tank.

The crankshaft was built-up and comprised a central cast-iron flywheel clamped between the cheeks of two half-cranks. Each of the latter was machined from a common steel forging and comprised mainshaft, flange with bobweight, crankpin and inner cheek. A combination of bolts and studs held the parts together, alignment being assured by their tight fit in their holes and a dowel. The crankpins were hollow, and a hole in the flywheel allowed the lubricating oil to reach both, while the chamber also acted as a sludge trap.

Each connecting rod and its cap were forged in light-alloy and fitted with steel-backed shell bearings. The caps were secured by locating bolts, retained by castle nuts and

Three-quarter rear view of the original McCandless prototype with monocoque rear pressings allied to tubular front section. Note rear number plate formed in seat base.

First of the Featherbed twin line as seen in the race paddock at the 1951 French Grand Prix at Albi.

locked with split pins once correctly tightened. The small-ends were fitted with phosphor-bronze bushes for the hollow gudgeon pins, which held the flat-topped pistons and were retained by circlips. Each piston had one scraper and two compression rings, was handed by the valve cutaways in its top, and gave a compression ratio of 6.7:1.

The pistons moved together in a one-piece, cast-iron cylinder block that was held to the crankcase by nine studs with nuts. It had cylinder spigots that ran down into the crankcase openings to a depth of 1 in., and

The prototype Model 88 Featherbed twin with its well valanced, sprung, front mudguard.

two pushrod tunnels at the front, which were spaced away from the cylinders to assist the air flow. The tappets were fitted in pairs into holes at the bottoms of the tunnels, each individual tappet being of semi-circular section and working against its partner. They were kept from turning by a plate between each pair, and this also stopped them from falling out when the block was lifted from the crankcase.

The cylinder head was cast in iron and had an integral rocker box. Each cylinder of the block had a small spigot that ran up into the head, and the joint was sealed by a copper-asbestos gasket. A combination of ten bolts and studs clamped the two parts together, some running up into the head and others down into the block. This arrangement made it awkward to remove the head with the engine in the frame and none too easy with it on the bench. However, it reduced the adverse effects of the fixings on air flow and cooling, while placing them in the best position for even clamping of the joint.

Lovely period picture showing Geoff Duke riding a Dominator 7 at Silverstone in 1952 and pacing cycle champion Jose Mieffret

The exhaust ports were widely splayed so that the cooling air could easily pass between them. The air was then guided, by the fins, to flow to each side, under the rocker box and over the combustion chamber, to exit at each side and the rear. This excellent cooling arrangement, with the airflow graduated across the hotter areas, was complemented by the angle, in plan, between the exhaust ports and the narrow valve angle.

Originally, on the inlet side of the cylinder head, there was a manifold cast as part of the head. This had a mounting face for the single Type 6 Amal carburettor of 1 in. bore and its separate, bottom-feed, float chamber. However, it was quickly changed to a design with twin parallel inlet ports in the cylinder head, and a separate light-alloy manifold, which was bolted to the head and supported the carburettor.

The combination of narrow valve angle, splayed exhaust ports and parallel inlets resulted in a compact combustion chamber in the modern style, and well in advance of most others of the period. It was this, plus the good cooling, that was to make the engine successful in a variety of fields and in different capacities over the years.

Each valve moved in a chilled, cast-iron guide, which was pressed in to a shoulder. Duplex valve springs were used, each pair being seated on a cup located on the valve guide, and retained by a collar and split collets. The rockers were nickel-steel forgings, and each oscillated on a fixed pin, these being angled to match the splay of the exhaust ports.

Early engines had rocker pins that were formed with an end flange, which was bolted to the cylinder head. This expensive construction was soon amended to a parallel pin, with an internal thread to assist extraction, and a machined slot in the outer end. The slot located on a plate, with depressions formed in it to suit, and a further outer plate

Aubrey Thompson of the RAC with his Model 7 and sidecar; a good ambassador for motorcycling who was much involved with rider training.

For 1953 the Model 7 was given a new frame with pivoted fork rear suspension and details to suit.

plus gaskets was fixed to the cylinder head using the original two bolt holes per rocker. The pins were a tight fit in the head, which made a threaded puller essential for removing them, while assembly called for care to align the slot with the plate and the plate to its fixings.

The rocker outer ends each carried an adjuster screw and locknut to set the valve gaps, access to these being provided by removable covers. There were two of these for the exhaust side, each held by two studs, but only a single cover for the two inlet valves, one stud and a dowel being provided to hold and locate it.

The inner rocker ends were each fitted with a hardened ball to match the hardened top cup of the appropriate pushrod. A light-gauge, high-tensile, steel tube was used for the pushrods with a hardened ball at the lower end as well as the cup at the top. Inlet and exhaust pushrods were of different lengths to suit the valve and rocker geometry, but all four sat in the tops of their respective tappets.

Below the tappets ran the camshaft, supported by a phosphor-bronze bush in each crankcase half. The left-hand end of the camshaft drove a timed breather whose fixed and running discs were ported and held in contact by a compression spring. The external exit from the discs was a drilling to the rear of the crankcase and then a pipe, while inside it was via the hollow camshaft to cross-holes.

The camshaft drive was in two sections, the first being a pinion fitted to the right-hand end of the crankshaft and meshed with a gear mounted on a spindle that was pressed into the timing chest wall of the crankcase. The gear ran at half engine speed, and integral with it were two chain sprockets. The outer of these drove the camshaft by a chain whose tension was set by an

Model 88 for 1954 with larger front brake but otherwise little altered.

adjustable slipper under its lower run.

The camshaft sprocket assembly included a large fibre gear, which drove the dynamo clamped to the front of the crankcase. The gear was not fixed to the sprocket, but was driven via a slipping clutch that could absorb shock loads. The small dynamo pinion meshed with the fibre gear, and the crankcase timing chest was extended forwards to enclose it, but with a hole in the wall to allow the pinion to pass through. This enabled the dynamo to be readily removed if desired.

The inner of the two sprockets that were integral with the intermediate camshaft gear drove the magneto. This was a flange-mounted Lucas K2F unit that was located behind the engine and fixed to the back of the timing chest, which was extended to accommodate it. The three magneto mounting studs had enough clearance in the flange holes to allow the chain to be adjusted for tension. An ignition auto-advance

The Model 7 Dominator for 1955 when it gained a light-alloy cylinder head and round tank badge.

mechanism was built into the magneto sprocket, and the complete assembly was held on the magneto armature taper by a self-extracting bolt. There was no key, so the timing depended on the fit of the taper, while undoing the securing bolt pulled the assembly off the shaft.

The oil pump for the dry-sump lubricating system was fitted into the timing chest below the crankshaft. It was a duplex gear pump driven by a worm nut on the end of the crankshaft and based on a design that dated back to 1931. While it worked well, it was also prone to allowing the oil tank contents to drain through it, although the firm always denied this. There was no anti-drain valve to prevent this until 1975, when it appeared for the last Commando engines, but the valve was never used for the Dominator.

The lubrication system began as an external oil tank, with a gauze filter on the supply line to the crankcase and then the pump. From the pump, a nipple took the oil into the timing cover, which had a pressure release valve in its rear edge. The cover was fitted with an oil seal that ran on the extreme right-hand end of the crankshaft so that the oil was forced, via drillings, to the seal housing and, thence, into the crankshaft.

Youthful show-time enthusiasm and dreams for a 1955 Model 88 with the new alloy cylinder head.

Oil from the big-ends lubricated the cylinder walls and this, plus oil released by the pressure valve, lu-

First enlargement for the twin was to this 596 cc Model 99. This one is in late 1956 form with AMC gearbox, new oil tank, 1957 silencers and revised headlamp shell.

bricated the rest of the lower half of the engine. The rocker box was lubricated from the oil return line, with a connection to two points in the top of the rocker box. After reaching the rocker spindles, the oil drained back to the crankcase down the pushrod tunnels, where it was collected with the rest by the scavenge side of the pump. One further connection was made to the rear edge of the timing cover. This came from the pressure side of the system and ran to a gauge set in the left-hand side of the petrol tank top.

The remainder of the machine came from the single-cylinder ES2 model, but with an improved gearbox. The transmission had a single-strand chain that took the drive from the engine sprocket, keyed on the crankshaft, to the multi-plate clutch at the gearbox. Chain tension was set by moving the gearbox. The clutch itself dated back to 1934 and included a shock-absorber in its centre.

The clutch drum included the sprocket and had friction inserts so that it acted as a plate. It ran on rollers held loosely in a cage, and had the other five friction plates splined to it. All the inserts were by Ferodo, so an oil shield was fitted round the drum to keep the oil at bay and the inserts dry.

Six plain plates were interleaved with the friction ones and splined to the clutch centre. A seventh plain plate went behind the clutch drum and carried the three studs on which were fitted the clutch springs, cups and securing bolts. The use of three springs to clamp the plates governed the use of three load and rebound rubbers in the centre shock absorber. Its three-vaned hub was splined to the gearbox mainshaft.

The clutch plates were lifted by a quick-thread mechanism mounted on the gearbox mainshaft axis at its right-hand end. The clutch cable was attached to a lever that turned the screw in its housing, and the motion was transmitted across to the pressure plate by a long pushrod and short mushroom. This mushroom had a large foot, and it was this, pushing on the pressure plate, that helped to lift the clutch cleanly, for it kept the plate square and prevented it from tilting.

The primary transmission was enclosed by a pressed-steel chaincase that was as old as the clutch. It was elegantly simple in design, with just an inner and outer held together by a single nut with a sealing band between the two halves. In fact, the inner was constructed from several parts with a rim running round near the edge of the back to take the sealing band. The outer was a deep pressing that used the draw angle of the press tool to provide the lead for the fit to the seal.

There were suitable pressings added to the chaincase to allow the footrest hanger to pass through it, for the gearbox shaft and to provide a cap to allow oil to be added and the chain tension checked. The single fixing nut was fitted to the footrest tube, and it was this that often led to oil leaks, due to it being overtightened and thus distorting the cover.

The four-speed gearbox design was as old as, or older than, the clutch and chaincase, for its origins went back to the early 1930s when Norton used Sturmey-Archer gearboxes made by their parent company, Raleigh. In 1934, Raleigh aban-

For 1957 the tank finish was changed to paint with separate plated side panels as shown by this Model 99.

The Model 77 first appeared in 1957 and was intended for sidecar work so used the older type frame with the 596 cc engine.

doned motorcycle production, including the gearboxes, so Norton took over the design, amended it a little, and had it made for them by Burman. In this form it was used by Norton from 1935, right through the war, and then experienced a minor change to the end cover for the post-war years.

During this period, the positive-stop mechanism was housed in an upward extension of the end covers, which resulted in the pedal pivot being rather too high and too far back. Thus, the pedal itself was really too long and had excessive travel when changing gear. The positive-stop mechanism was linked to the camplate by external levers and a rod, which gave problems due to wear or poor adjustment.

This form of gearbox was difficult to accommodate with the twin-cylinder engine, so it was revised by moving the change mechanism to a point in front of the gearbox shafts. This allowed it to be directly linked to the camplate and, furthermore, resulted in the pedal pivot being better placed to give a shorter pedal and movement.

The revised gearbox became known as the 'laid-down' type and was soon used by most of the Norton range. In the change, the opportunity was also taken to improve the gearbox shell, so this light-alloy casting was clamped between frame members. Previously, its double lugs had been prone to wear, if the fixings were left slack, and then could fracture when they were tightened.

Inside the shell was a very conventional, and very good, gearbox. The mainshaft was above the layshaft and the sleeve gear concentric with the mainshaft. Ball races supported the sleeve gear, the right-hand end of the mainshaft and the left-hand end of the layshaft, while there were bronze bushes for the other end of the layshaft and some of the gears. The sleeve gear had both a bush and a row of uncaged rollers to support the mainshaft, plus a pen-steel washer to keep the oil inside.

The gears were selected by a pair of forks that were mounted on a single cross-rod and controlled by a circular camplate. This part included a small pinion, which meshed with a quadrant that was linked to the positive-stop mechanism. The mechanism continued to be the double-pawl-and-ratchet type, despite its new location, and terminated in a foot pedal on the right-hand side of the machine.

Two end covers on the right enclosed the gears, with the positive-stop mechanism between them, and the inner supported the kick-start spindle. This carried a pawl that engaged in an internal ratchet cut in the layshaft first gear. A boss was provided in the inner cover for the clutch cable adjuster, and a small cover in the outer for clutch screw adjustment and to act as a gearbox oil filler.

The engine and gearbox were mounted in a cradle frame, with plunger rear suspension, using front and rear engine plates. The frame was constructed from tubes that were brazed into forged lugs with single top, down and saddle tubes. A cradle beneath the engine extended back as two tubes to the rear plunger lugs, the tops of which were joined to the top and saddle tubes by two further tubes. In true Norton fashion, it was massive, strong and heavy.

The plunger rear suspension comprised a near vertical rod on each side, which was held in a socket

Rebuilt Model 99 of 1957 with its distinctive lines in a more modern paddock along with an older Douglas.

in the bottom of the plunger lug and clamped at the top. A slider and wheel spindle assembly moved up and down on each rod, and were controlled by bump and rebound springs above and below the slider, with covers to enclose them. There was grease lubrication, but no damping, other than that provided by friction.

A version of the Dominator with a rigid frame was also projected, as many sidecar drivers preferred this arrangement to any form of rear suspension. For this, Norton would have simply taken their stock, rigid cradle-frame, as used by the models 16H, Big 4 and 18, and fitted the twin engine and gearbox. In fact, although mocked-up, none was thought to have been built.

At the front of the frame went Roadholder telescopic forks with two-way hydraulic damping. The forks pivoted in cup-and-cone bearings and were of straightforward construction, having external springs under shrouds, the upper of which incorporated headlamp shell mountings. A friction steering damper was provided, the friction discs being beneath the lower crown and the control knob above the top one.

Both wheels had offset hubs and 7 in. single-leading-shoe brakes, with each brake shoe mounted on its own pivot pin. The front wheel had a one-piece hub and drum, which was spoked into a 21 in. steel rim fitted with a 3.00 in. section tyre. The rear wheel had the brake drum bolted to the hub and the assembly revolved on a one-piece spindle, so it was without the quickly-detachable facility of the past. It, too, had a steel rim, but the tyre size was 3.50 x 19 in. The speedometer drive was taken from the right-hand end of the hub.

Timing side of the 1957 Model 77 showing its different shape of oil tank compared with the Featherbed twins.

Good touring mudguards were fitted to both wheels, the front being supported by a bridge plus front and rear stays, of which the rear

Drive side of the 1957 Model 88 Featherbed twin with the Norton pressed-steel chaincase as used by them for many years.

doubled as the front stand. There was also a centre stand and an optional prop stand that was bolted to the left-hand front engine plate. The rear mudguard was of similar section to the front and supported by two stays on each side, one of which was formed as a lifting handle.

The remainder of the machine followed traditional British lines, so there was a saddle, which was adjustable for height. Pillion footrests were listed, but no pad, so the Norton owner was free to choose from proprietary makes. The oil tank went below the saddle on the right-hand side of the machine and was matched by the battery on the left-hand side. A toolbox went between the right-hand side chainstays, just in front of the plunger unit.

An exhaust system went on each side of the machine, the pipe being clamped into the port by a large finned nut, which was never easy to keep tight. Each pipe swept down to a low-level tubular silencer with tailpipe. The 3¾ gallon petrol tank had its filler on the right-hand side, to match the oil pressure gauge, and was fitted with kneegrips. The other instruments were the speedometer, which was in a fork-top panel, and the ammeter, which went with the light switch in a small panel in the headlamp shell. The horn was hung from the left-hand side saddle-spring lug, and the hand and foot controls were conventional.

The bulk of the finish was in black, but the petrol tank was chrome-plated with silver panels on the top and each side. The panels were lined with an outer black line and thin inner red one in traditional Norton style. The wheel rims were chrome-plated with black centres and lined red, except for show and road test models, which had the centres in silver.

In this form, the Dominator went on sale and, at first, was for export only, although a few machines reached the home market during 1949. Their owners were generally very pleased with their purchase, for the twin proved to be fast, have good acceleration, a nice gear change and handling to inspire confidence. If the model lacked anything, it was in the braking department, for this was barely adequate for the machine's performance. This was hardly surprising, for the brakes came from the slower singles, and even the camshaft-engined Internationals lacked the speed of the twin when carrying full road equipment.

With production the main need,

A Model 99 from 1958 as rebuilt in the 1980s during the classic bike revival.

The 1958 Nomad off-road model with 596 cc engine housed in Model 77 cycle parts adapted with small tank, short seat and suitable tyres and mudguards.

there were few, if any, changes for 1950, although a few export models were built with Polychromatic blue or Post Office red tank panels in place of the usual silver. There was a revision to the front brake for 1951. The hub was changed to a design with a cast-iron brake drum, which was riveted to the hub. The diameter was unchanged, but the backplate became a polished light-alloy casting. This improved the looks, but otherwise the Model 7 continued as it was.

For 1952, it was to be joined by a new version, which was to carry the twin on in a much more famous form. The Model 7 stayed as it was, except that the nickel shortage led to the petrol tank being finished in silver all over, the panels being outlined by the black and red lining. During the year, the wheel rim centre colour was changed to silver, but the lining continued in red.

Featherbed

Harold Daniell gave the new frame of the 1950 works Nortons its 'Featherbed' name due to the comfortable ride it gave him. It replaced the old plunger frame, known in racing form as 'the garden gate', and, while not the first frame with a pivoted rear fork, it was to become the standard against which the rest were measured for a long, long time.

The Featherbed frame had its roots in Ireland where Rex and Cromie McCandless sowed its seeds during the war and just after. Artie Bell, a works Norton rider of the late 1940s, was involved with them, and from this early work, Rex built up a detailed knowledge of suspension systems and frame design. In time, this, and an expertise with carburettors, led to an association with Norton and, late in 1949, a brief to design and make a new frame.

The result was classically simple with two main frame loops that joined at the headstock. The top and downtubes crossed over just behind this area, and cross-tubes braced the loops, all joints being sif-bronze welded. The subframe was

Bernal Osborne with a Nomad during a press workout in 1958. It took muscle to handle the weight and power over a scrambles course.

The De Luxe versions of the Featherbed came in for 1960 with the slimline frame and enclosure. This is the Model 99dl.

bolted in place and simply supported the tops of the McCandless rear units and the seat. The rear fork pivoted between long gusset plates welded into the lower corner of each main loop and, thus, was very well supported.

Fitted with a works engine, the Featherbed was first seen at the Blandford circuit, in April 1950, where Geoff Duke won the 500 cc race with ease. The factory team dominated both Junior and Senior TTs that year, and the public were clamouring for the new frame. It went on the production Manx for 1951, and during that year, the model many craved for was seen at Assen, a twin engine in the Featherbed frame.

Late in 1951, the new machine was officially announced as the Model 88 Dominator but, sadly, for buyers at home, it was export only at first. It used a production version of the Featherbed frame, made from a commercial grade of steel tubing, with the rear fork pivoted on Silentbloc bushes. The subframe continued to be bolted on and was controlled by spring units with hydraulic damping.

The front forks were the Manx type, which was a shorter version of the Roadholders, and they pivoted in angular-contact ball bearings in the headstock. The forks had internal springs and two-way hydraulic damping, but no steering damper. The engine, gearbox and primary drive were standard units that were built up into an assembly. This was installed in the frame in mounting plates and was attached to it at three points. The rest of the machine was far more modern than the Model 7, and the details reflected this.

In its original Rex McCandless prototype form, built in 1951, the Featherbed twin was even more modern and way in advance of its contemporaries. It used the normal Featherbed front loops, to which was attached a monocoque rear structure that acted as a deep rear mudguard and dualseat support. The rear number plate was formed in the rear of the seat base, with the rear light a long, thin slot in the metal above it. Within the monocoque went the oil tank, and under the seat there was space for the tools.

The petrol tank was shaped to blend in with the monocoque, and there was further innovation at the front, where a cowling at the top of the forks flowed down into the shrouds. The cowling carried the speedometer in its top as well as the headlight unit, while beneath the light was an area for the front number plate. Fixed to the cowling was the deeply valanced and sprung front mudguard.

Road test shot of the 99 De Luxe which swung round the bends as well as ever although both wide and slim frames have their adherents.

In an earlier experiment, this frame type was modified to accommodate a 600 cc, four-cylinder, water-cooled, Fiat car engine. The crankshaft ran in-line, and Norton claimed that it would not work due to torque reaction, but McCandless disproved this by using a machine with a tuned, in-line, Sunbeam twin engine in a Manx frame.

Norton would have none of the monocoque, so the Model 88 had the same Featherbed layout as the racing machines. In its original 1952 form, it did have a well valanced, sprung front mudguard, but this

In contrast to the De Luxe models, the Sports Special versions were introduced in 1961 and this is the 99SS.

rather detracted from its looks. The top of the forks carried a small fascia panel, which held the speedometer, ammeter and light switch, while, from the start, the Model 88 was fitted with an underslung pilot lamp. This was used for parking, as it was nearly invisible when on the move.

Also new for 1961 was the 646 cc Manxman, here seen in its original export guise with raised bars.

Staff members from *The Motor Cycle* demonstrating riding gear in 1954 for an article. The Model 7 s

has had an airscoop added to its front brake and the solo is a Model 88.

Early in 1962 the engine was stretched again to 745 cc for the export Atlas which later reached its home market.

The silencers had a new shape, being elliptical in section and of megaphone style with reverse cone and tailpipe when viewed from the side. They became known as 'the pear-shape silencers'. The Model 88 inherited the petrol tank type and mounting from the Manx, so the tank sat on rubber pads on the frame top tubes and was held down by a strap, hinged at the front. Behind the 3½ gallon tank went a nice dualseat, which was held in place by two thumb-screws.

Beneath the dualseat went the tooltray, and below that the oil tank and battery, which both sat on a platform above the gearbox. The front hub was as for the Model 7, but the rear became quickly-detachable. Both brakes remained at the 7 in. size, while the front tyre became 3.25 x 19 in. The result was a much lighter machine.

Right at the start, the Model 88 had a black frame, but this soon changed to the metallic grey that was applied to all painted parts of the machine. The petrol tank was chrome-plated with grey panels, lined in black and red, while the wheel rims were also plated with the centres in grey and lined in red. During the year, the wheel rim grey changed to silver, while some export models had blue tank panels lined in black and white.

There were limited changes for the Model 88 for 1953, with a move to Armstrong rear suspension units and a 3.00 in. front tyre section. For Norton diehards, the grey finish was joined by an optional one in black and silver on the lines of the Model 7. That machine was given a major face-lift, perhaps to appease home market buyers who could not get their hands on the Featherbed twin.

The revised Model 7 Dominator changed to a frame with pivoted-fork rear suspension, but based on the old plunger type. Thus, it continued with the tube and brazed-lug form of construction and the single top and downtubes. There were hydraulically-damped Armstrong spring units to control the new fork which, again, moved on Silentbloc bushes. The rear mudguard was new and a rather flat dualseat was fitted as standard. The oil gauge was dropped, while the pear-shaped silencers were adopted, as was the underslung pilot lamp. The front tyre changed to 3.25 x 19 in., and the rear hub to the quickly-detachable type of the Model 88. The finish was as in late 1952.

One more variant of the Dominator was built in 1953, but this was a one-off and had a side-valve engine. It was produced for the army, and the aim was to persuade the services to change from the Triumph TRW they were then using, but this was an optimistic idea that overlooked the spares holding already in army stores.

The Dominator engine, with its forward camshaft, lent itself to the exercise, and the major work concerned a new head and block. The new top half replaced the standard one with a cast-iron block, which had the valves at the front and the Amal carburettor at the rear. The one-piece head was a light-alloy casting, and the joint between it and the block was angled to improve the combustion chamber shape. The inlet tract ran between the cylinder bores, and the front exhaust pipes

A De Luxe version of the 650, as the Manxman became known in its home country, was built, but only for 1962.

The sporting 650SS version of the twin proved very popular and performed well, this being the home market model for 1962-63.

joined to feed a single silencer mounted low down on the left.

One area of the service model that was new for Norton was an alternator, rectifier and coil ignition, with a distributor replacing the normal magneto. The primary chaincase was in cast-alloy, rather than

The 1963 650SS twin fitted with the usual flat handlebars for the home market.

the usual pressed steel, and a 'laid-down' gearbox was fitted. The frame was a shortened rigid one from the single-cylinder 16H model and was fitted with Roadholder front forks. The petrol tank came from the 500T trials model, the wheels were stock, and there was a saddle rather than a dualseat.

The machine was built, demonstrated, rejected and, finally discarded at the Bracebridge Street works. Years later, it was restored by Sammy Miller for his museum, so it now lives on in the nice grey of the Featherbed twin, rather than its original drab khaki.

Back with the mainstream twins, the only change for both models for 1954 was to a larger 8 in. front brake, which continued in an offset hub. Rather more happened for 1955, as both models changed to a light-alloy cylinder head and went over to a Monobloc carburettor. They also had a new, round-plastic tank badge, and the rear number plate was boxed in.

The dualseats on both machines were new, but the Featherbed model continued to differ from that fitted to the Dominator 7, whose seat was common to the road singles. The Model 88 had additional changes, and its subframe was welded in place instead of being bolted on. Full-width, light-alloy hubs were adopted by both wheels and, although the brake size remained as before, the hubs were ribbed for strength and cooling. The rear wheel remained quickly-detachable, and the tyre sizes were unchanged.

At the end of the 1955 season, the Model 7 Dominator was dropped, but the time had come for further changes and a larger engine.

Publicity shot of the 650SS taken in 1963 when the cigarette was socially acceptable in such pictures.

More capacity

During the 1950s, most British 500 cc twins were joined by a larger version to meet the cry, often originating in the USA, for more power. While this could be, and often was, wrung from the smaller twin, there is no substitute for cubes, and the export markets preferred the larger engine. This gave the power, plus more low- and mid-range torque, while pulling a higher gear and giving an easier ride.

Norton's response was the Model 99, which duplicated the 88, except in capacity, carburettor and gearing. The capacity was 596 cc and came from 68 x 82 mm dimensions, while the Monobloc fitted was of 1-1/16 in. bore. The compression ratio of the new engine was 7.4:1, and the

A 1963 Norton twin fitted with the Avonair fairing which was offered for the SS models, with a view to production racing.

The Atlas MX scrambles model of 1964 with twin-carburettor engine in AMC frame but with Norton forks and wheels. Hard work!

88 engine also had a rise in ratio to 7.8:1. In other respects, the 99 was as the 88.

Both models had some changes on the cycle side, with a new oil tank whose shape and style was matched by a battery container on the left. The underslung pilot light went, unmourned, and so did the fascia panel at the top of the forks. Its job was taken over by a panel that was fitted into the top of a deeper headlamp shell and which carried the speedometer, ammeter and light switch. The finish continued in the chrome-plating and grey, but a small, round, plastic Norton badge appeared in the timing cover.

In May of 1956, the gearbox was revised and its manufacture transferred to the AMC works at Plumstead. Norton had become part of the AMC group some years earlier, and the intention was to fit a common gearbox to all AJS, Matchless and Norton singles and twins of 350 cc or more. This came to pass, although there were often minor variations in shell lugs or mainshaft lengths, and the gearbox continued in use until the late 1970s on Norton Commando twins.

The revised gearbox was known as the 'AMC type' and had the clutch-lift and positive-stop mechanisms altered. The clutch-lift became a shaped arm, which was pulled by the cable to move the pushrod. Unfortunately, the design called for an adjuster screw in the pressure

A 1964 650SS being smartened up for sale among a dealer's stock of secondhand machines.

plate and no clutch mushroom, so the plate was no longer kept square when lifted, other than by careful adjustment of the springs.

The positive-stop mechanism only differed in the ratchet design, but from then on was effectively as before. Inside the gearbox, there were detail alterations only, and the same applied to the clutch and the shock absorber in its centre. The end covers were new and shorter, so the AMC gearbox was easy to distinguish from the older Burman-built type.

There were only detail changes to the 88 and 99 models for 1957, when tubular silencers without tail-pipes replaced the pear-shaped ones. There was also a gradual changeover to Girling rear suspension units. The front hub, cylinder head and footrests were all new, but the changes were small. The hub had its iron drum cast in place instead of being bolted, the head had more finning between the exhaust ports, and the footrests lost their traditional half-moon section to become round and plain.

The headlamp was altered, so the instruments and switch were mounted directly in the shell, rather than on the separate panel. The finish continued in grey, but the petrol tank style was altered, and it was painted all over with separate chrome-plated side panels. These sat on plastic mats and were secured by the tank badge and kneegrip on each side.

The two models with the Featherbed frame were joined by a third for 1957, this being the 596 cc Model 77. This was introduced for sidecar drivers as, at that time, it was thought that the Featherbed frame was not suited to this work and the unusual loads it placed on the machine.

The 77 used the standard 99 engine and gearbox in a frame with pivoted-fork rear suspension that was based on that used by the late Model 7. Thus, it was of brazed-tube-and-lug construction with single top and downtubes, and it came with sidecar lugs. Roadholder telescopic forks went at the front, and both wheels had the full-width, light-alloy hubs with the same brake sizes as the other models. Tyre sections were 3.25 in. front and 3.50 in. rear, both on 19 in. rims. The headlight shell was as for the 1956 twins with the separate panel, and the oil tank and combined toolbox and battery compartment were styled to fit in with the new frame. A flat, uncompromising dualseat, which looked as inviting as a plank, was supplied, and the model came with the new silencers and a 3 gallon petrol tank.

Atlas Norton twin out on the road in 1964; there was little difference between the various Featherbed models.

The finish was as for the other twins, or in black and silver.

There were no changes to the 77 for 1958, but the 88 and 99 went over to an alternator, coil ignition and a distributor in place of the magneto. An ignition switch appeared in the centre of the lighting one, and the Lucas RM15 alternator was spigoted to the left-hand crankcase within the primary chaincase. The distributor included an auto-advance mechanism, so it was driven by a simple sprocket, and both the crankcase and timing cover were amended to take account of the removal of the dynamo. A cover was added over the front engine plates.

The three road models were joined by the 99 Nomad, which was built for the American enduro market as a scrambler with lights. It used the 596 cc engine, with the compression ratio raised to 9.0:1, twin Type 276 carburettors and a siamesed exhaust system. It retained the magneto for ignition, but had a Lucas RM13/15 alternator to power the lights.

The Nomad used the frame from the 77, as the width of the lower tubes of the Featherbed made it unsuitable for off-road work. It had an undershield to protect the crankcase, Roadholder forks and a 21 in. front wheel. Trail tyres were fitted, along with light-alloy mudguards and a 2¼ gallon petrol tank. The

The N15CS of 1968, which was derived from the Atlas scrambler, and retained the Norton forks and wheels with the AMC frame.

Careful inspection of a 1965 Atlas before a decision, maybe between the Norton and the Triumph beside it.

finish was black, the tank being red with chrome-plated side panels, while the mudguards and lower fork legs were polished. The seat top was white, so the whole ensemble had style and colour to make it stand out.

The advent of twin carburettors

Show time, and a 1965 650SS in all its black and chrome glory to tempt the customers.

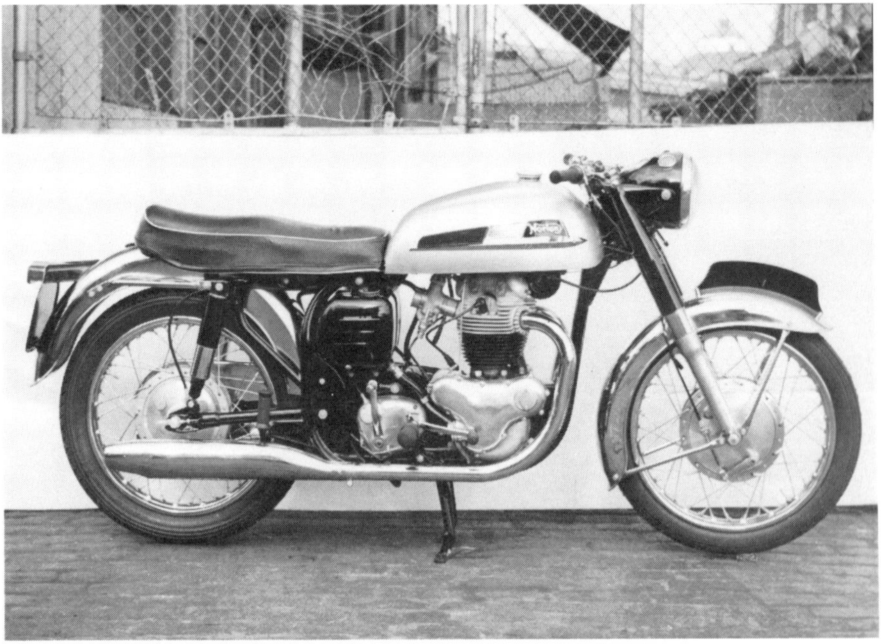

For those who preferred a 500, Norton offered the 88SS up to 1966, the year this one came from.

for the Nomad brought a clamour for the same option for the road models. This was met early in 1958, when the twin Amals and 9.0:1 pistons were listed as options just in time for the Thruxton 500 mile race.

Further options for the 88 and 99 arrived later that year, along with

The Atlas was available to the police in white, with equipment to suit its varied duties.

A 1966 Atlas out on test. By then, vibration, inherent in the vertical twin and increased in effect by the larger capacity, was becoming a problem.

the death knell of the 77. This came about because the great Eric Oliver took a fairly standard 88, hitched it to a road Watsonian Monaco sidecar, added forks with special crowns, and proceeded to finish 10th in the sidecar TT. In due course, the fork options, plus heavy-duty springs and a steering damper, were on the list, so there was no further need for the 77, which was duly dropped.

For 1959, the 88 and 99 were treated to a new camshaft and a further option in the form of a full rear chaincase. The standard finish continued in the grey, but there were options of Metalescent blue, Post Office red, or the traditional Norton black and silver. Chrome-plated mudguards were a further option to brighten the looks of the twins.

Variations for the 1960s

The Norton twin range doubled in size for 1960, when both the 88 and 99 became available with rear enclosure styling, and a smaller version of the Nomad was added to the line-up. The new road models were listed as de luxe versions, so the existing ones became the standard models, having carried a 'de luxe' tag since 1956.

The enclosure was the main talking point of the new models and was based on that of the 249 cc Jubilee twin, which had been introduced late in 1958. To enable the panels to fit the larger twins, the Featherbed frame was modified by bringing the main loops closer together in the region of the dualseat nose and tank end. This change was said to be in the interests of rider comfort, as it allowed both seat and tank to be narrower, and it was promoted in this manner in the firm's brochure.

The new frame soon became known as the 'slimline' so, invariably, the earlier type became the 'wideline', and the names have stuck ever since. The rear enclosure ran back from the cylinder head to the

Another Atlas on test. This time, a 1967 model, but little altered from earlier examples.

The P11 introduced in 1967 with the Atlas engine in a Matchless G85CS frame fitted with AMC forks and wheels.

rear number plate and down from the dualseat to the silencers, except for a cut-out that left most of the rear wheel in view. It was much as the Triumph twin's bathtub enclosure, but had its own line to distinguish it.

The rear enclosure extended far enough forward to cover the carburettor, although its presence inhibited the use of twin instruments. It was built up from two side panels, which were held in place by Dzus quarter-turn fasteners. The tail section was bolted in place to double as the rear mudguard, and the number plate could be detached to let the rear wheel roll out. A lifting handle was provided on the left-hand side of the enclosure.

For 1960 a new dualseat was introduced for both standard and de luxe twins. This had locating pegs at the front and springclips at the rear. The de luxe models had a more deeply valanced front mudguard, but all had new silencers, still without tailpipes, and a new 3.6 gallon petrol tank. This had restyled tank badges, which were long and slim with small kneegrips incorporated in their ends. They also acted as dividers for the two-tone finish, which was adopted by all the models.

At first, it seemed that all, or most, colours were available for all models, but this soon changed to a more limited choice. For the de luxe twins, the first colour, which could be red, blue or Forest green, was applied to the upper petrol tank, headlamp shell, top fork shrouds and upper part of the rear enclosure. The second colour was called Dove grey, but looked more like cream,and was used for the rest of the painted parts, which included the frame.

The standard twins had their first colour, which could be red, black or metallic grey, applied to the frame, chainguard, oil tank and toolbox, as well as the upper petrol tank and upper forks, while the second colour was again the Dove grey. For all the twins, the hubs were left natural, with polished backplates and cover plates, and the wheel rims were chrome-plated.

All the changes that appeared for the de luxe twins also applied to the standard models, although their frames lacked the enclosure brackets. For all engines, there was an increase in compression ratio, the 88 rising to 8.1:0 and the 99 to 7.6:1.

The final new model for 1960 was the 88 Nomad, which simply duplicated the larger version, but used a tuned 88 engine, coil ignition and twin, 1 in. bore, carburettors. Its finish was as for the 99 Nomad, and both had a chrome-plated chaincase. Neither was to run on past the end of the year so, for the time being, large-capacity off-road twins were not to be found in the Norton list.

Drive side of a 1967 P11 showing the cast alloy primary chaincase and the neat installation of the exhaust pipe above it.

This left the standard and de luxe 88 and 99 twins to go forward for 1961. The engines had another increase in compression ratio to 8.5:1 for the 88 and 8.25:1 for the 99, while the rear seat fastening was changed to a Dzus quarter-turn type. Finishes continued to be two-tone, but in specific colours for each model. Thus, the standard 88 was in green,

Last year for the Atlas was 1968 when it had a dualseat with hump but retained the Norton twin line seen for many years.

the de luxe in red, the standard 99 in metallic grey and the de luxe 99 in blue, all with Dove grey as the second colour.

This smaller range soon began to increase in numbers, for it was joined by an even faster twin listed, initially, for the American market only. The machine was the Manxman, which had an enlarged, 646 cc engine with dimensions of 68 x 89 mm. The compression ratio was 8.3:1 and there were twin 1-1/8 in. Amal carburettors on downdraught inlet tracts. A rev-counter drive went on the timing cover and was driven from the camshaft, while the engine had magneto ignition and a siamesed exhaust. It went into the standard Featherbed cycle parts but, for the USA, the tyre sizes were 3.25 x 19 in. front and 4.00 x 18 in. rear. The finish was in Polychromatic blue and grey on the lines of the standard twins, but with chrome-plating for the mudguards and chaincase.

Early in 1961, the Manxman went on show in Europe, where it lost its US-style handlebars, was fitted with the same tyres as the other twins, and was finished in two-tone grey. It was listed simply as the '650' and was joined, in April, by two new sports special models in the form of the 88SS and 99SS.

Both these were based heavily on the existing standard models, but had twin carburettors of 1-1/16

The same cycle parts were used by the 650SS for 1968 when it still had the twin carburettors and the rev-counter.

in. bore, polished internals and a hotter camshaft. On the outside went a siamesed exhaust system, ball-ended control levers and a folding kickstart. The rev-counter was an option, as were rearsets, for the trends were moving away from touring and enclosure towards performance and café racers. Finishes were green and Dove grey for the 88SS and two-tone grey for the 99SS on the lines of the standard models.

Late in 1961, the 650 reached its home market as part of the 1962 range, and the standard model was joined by de luxe and SS versions. All three had a new cylinder head with downdraught inlet ports, but the standard and de luxe models only had a single 1-1/8 in. carburettor. The 650SS was fitted with twin 1-1/16 in. instruments, in line with the other SS models, while all the 650s ran an 8.9:1 compression ratio.

The 88SS also had the new cylinder head with downdraught ports, which boosted performance, but could make cold starting tricky. Petrol could easily run down the tracts into the engine, so it flooded if it failed to fire on the first prod. Owners soon learned not to flood the carburettors or, if they did, how to push start the twin. For the 88SS, the compression ratio went up to 9.5:1 and it was fitted with a magneto with manual advance.

All nine models, in three capacities and three build styles, had a great deal in common. The 99SS had to make do with the older cylinder head with splayed inlet ports and kept to coil ignition. All the SS models were fitted with Avon GP rear tyres and, during the year, all models switched over to RM19 alternators. Colours were as for 1961, the 650 being in grey, de luxe 650 in blue and Dove grey, and the 650SS in black with a silver tank and the option of chrome-plated mudguards.

In March 1962, a further, export-only, model joined the range as the 745 cc Atlas. This was much as the others, but obtained its power from 73 x 89 mm dimensions, a 7.6:1 compression ratio and single 1-1/16 in. carburettor. A magneto was used for ignition, and the engine breather was modified to an elbow at the left-hand end of the camshaft, rather than a pipe from the rear of the crankcase. For the USA, the machine had a small petrol tank and high-rise handlebars, but the finish was as for the 650SS, except that the chrome-plated mudguards were standard.

The range was drastically pruned at the end of 1962, when all three versions of the 99, the de luxe 88 and de luxe 650 models were dropped. Enclosure was out and sports specification in! This left standard and SS models in 88 and 650 sizes, plus the Atlas, all of which went forward for 1963 with some colour changes. The Atlas and 650SS stayed as they were, the 88SS copied the larger sports twin, the 88 was in green and off-

For 1968 the P11A was built with low level exhausts and tilted silencers for its 745 cc engine. In its last few months it was known as the Ranger.

white, while the 650 was in Polychromatic blue and black. The last two also had the option of the chrome-plated mudguards.

In August 1963, Norton returned to the off-road market with the Atlas scrambler, the first of the hybrids. During the previous year, the motorcycle world had been shocked by the news that the Bracebridge Street factory was to close and production moved to Plumstead, alongside the AMC models. This duly came to pass, and for many Norton enthusiasts it was the end, for Bracebridge Street meant Norton to them, even if the factory and plant were old, tired and decrepit in most respects.

Such moves seldom work too well, as much expertise is lost in the process that the accountants fail to allow for. Due to the concentration of production, management began to move towards a rationalisation policy so that group parts would be used in place of traditional ones.

The scramble Atlas was a foretaste of this, having a twin-carburettor engine and AMC gearbox installed in the AMC sports twin frame. Norton forks, wheels and brakes were used, with a seat and silencers from the AMC twin, and the petrol tank from a scrambler. The machine was fitted with trail tyres and also with full road equipment, including a rev-counter.

The Mercury which continued alone for 1969 with a single-carburettor 646 cc engine in the familiar cycle parts.

The works Domiracer ridden into third place in the 1961 Senior TT by Tom Phillis.

The road range was thinned down further at the end of 1963, when the 88 and 650 were dropped, the former after more than a decade of service. This left the two SS machines, plus the Atlas and its scrambles derivative, the last two still being for export only. All models had new fork crowns, which spaced out the legs to allow the fitment of a fatter tyre, steering locks and 12 volt electrics. The Atlas went over to twin carburettors and, early in 1964, finally reached its home market. For that, it had the same cycle parts and finish as the 650SS which now, along with the 88SS, had the chrome-plated mudguards fitted as standard and black ones as an option. The Atlas made do without that choice, but could have a red or black petrol tank in place of the silver.

During the year, the Atlas scrambler became the N15CS'N', and the four models continued for 1965 with a wider rear chain and a Cherry red petrol tank for the Atlas. The hybrids also began to appear as AJS or Matchless twins, but using Norton Atlas engines, forks and brakes, which confused the public and reflected the growing financial problems of the AMC group.

The four Norton models continued as they were for 1966, except for a change to Burgundy for the Atlas tank. The AMC hybrids also ran on but, during the year, AMC, including Norton, failed and were bought out by Manganese Bronze Holdings. From this came, in time, Norton-Villiers and the decision to design and build the Norton Commando to combat the vibration of the Atlas engine. This had reached an unacceptable level, and the Commando was to run on through the 1970s and, thus, take over from the Featherbed Norton.

Before this happened, the existing range had further changes to go through, and hybrids were to come and go, sometimes in a matter of months. For 1967, the 650SS and Atlas changed to an RM21 alternator and twin 930 Amal Concentric carburettors, but the 88SS was dropped, so a further link with the past was severed. The two models were both fitted with matching speedometer and rev-counter and, as these went on a plate held by the fork top nuts, the light switch was fitted between them.

The off-road N15CS'N' continued, and the range was joined by the P11 in March 1967. This had the twin-carburettor Atlas engine, with capacitor ignition, fitted in a Matchless G85CS scrambles frame. The front forks and hubs were both AMC items, so the brake sizes were 7 in. for both front and rear wheels, which were shod with 3.25 x 19 in. and 4.00 x 18 in. tyres respectively. The P11 had a waist-level exhaust pipe and silencer on each side, a 2¼ gallon petrol tank, and a Candy Apple red finish. The primary chaincase was in cast-alloy, held together by many screws, and the model was fitted with an undershield, prop stand and lights. The mudguards were polished light-alloy, both speedometer and rev-counter (reading to 120 mph and 8000 rpm) were fitted, and the combination of short dualseat, neat side covers and bright finish gave the model real style.

For 1968, the two road models continued as they were, except for a

Sid Mizen seated on the Domiracer minus its fairing. The machine which should have succeeded the Manx.

capacitor ignition system and a hump for the seat, while the off-road twins became the N15CS and P11A. In neither case did this make much difference, for the first kept to the Norton forks and hubs, while the second stuck to the AMC components. Both were street-legal with lights and silencers, of which those for the P11A were repositioned. The exhaust pipes were changed to being down-swept, and the silencers were tilted up and of a new form with small reverse-cone ends.

Near the end of the year, the P11A was renamed the Ranger, but it was dropped, together with the N15CS and the Atlas, before the year was out. This left the 650SS to continue alone, as the sole twin with the Featherbed frame, for the rest of the range had the new Commando type.

The lone model was renamed the Mercury and reverted to a single 930 carburettor. The seat was revised and the mudguards, oil tank, toolbox and primary chaincase were in Atlantic blue, but the tank was still in silver and the frame and forks black in true Norton style. There was no rev-counter, so the earlier twin-instrument mounting plate was used with the speedometer on the right and light switch to the left. Side reflectors were added, and stainless-steel mudguards offered as an option.

In this way, the Mercury ran on into 1970 with a rev-counter option and chrome-plated mudguards as standard, but then it came to its end. Some two decades had passed since Joe Craig had unveiled the Featherbed for Geoff Duke to ride at Blandford, and many riders were sorry that it was no more.

Some kept the frame, but not the engine, to create the Triton, or a similar café-racer-style model. This concept dated from the 1950s and, while most fitted the Triumph twin engine, other power units were installed over the years. Not all used the twin frame; in fact, more came to have a staid Model 50 as the donor machine, but this made no real difference, other than to cost.

In one way or another, the Featherbed Norton twin lived on, while its roots in the early Dominator continued to nourish the Commando.

Twins in competition

Norton racing efforts concentrated on their works singles, but the twins did play their part in the story, with occasional appearances on the sporting scene in the 1950s. These ranged from the Clubman's TT at home to the sand-and-road circuit of Daytona,and the ISDT somewhere in Europe.

Eric Oliver showed the sidecar way in 1958, and in 1961, the Domiracer, as it became known, ran well to a third place in the Senior TT. During the 1960s, the twin became successful in the major production races and, in this period, Paul Dunstall had many successes with his riders on 500 and 650 twins. Dunstall was the major tuner for the twins at that time, and his machines,

Brian Setchell, here in the 1964 Thruxton 500 mile race, with the 1962 650SS which won in 1962, 1963 and 1964.

Joe Dunphy on the Dunstall Dominator which enjoyed many racing successes during the 1960s.

in racing and road forms, were highly successful.

The Norton mantle was then taken over by the Commando and, with this model, ran on for several more years. However, its engine was the Atlas, which could trace its line straight back to the original Model 7. All owed their success to the fine combustion chamber and engine layout first schemed by Bert Hopwood. Truly, it was one of the great motorcycle designs.

Dominator Specifications

All models had twin cylinders, overhead valves, telescopic front forks and a four-speed gearbox. All had pivoted-fork rear suspension, except the Model 7 for 1949-52, which had a plunger frame.

Model	7	88	88 Nomad	88SS	77	99
years	1949-55	1952-63	1960	1961-66	1957-58	1956-62
bore mm	66	66	66	66	68	68
stroke mm	72.6	72.6	72.6	72.6	82	82
capacity cc	497	497	497	497	596	596
comp. ratio	6.7	6.7[1]	8.1	8.5[2]	7.4	7.4[3]
ignition	mag	mag[4]	coil	coil[5]	mag	mag[4]
generator	dynamo	dynamo[6]	alt	alt	dynamo	dynamo[6]
carb type	276[7]	276[7]	376 (2)	376 (2)	376	376
carb size	1	1	1	1-1/16	1-1/16	1-1/16
top gear	5.00	5.00[8]	5.00	5.00[9]	4.53	4.53[10]
petrol - gall	3.75	3.5[11]	2.25	3.6	3.0	3.5[11]
front tyre	3.00x21[12]	3.25x19[13]	3.00x21	3.00x19	3.25x19	3.25x19
rear tyre	3.50x19	3.50x19	4.00x19	3.50x19	3.50x19	3.50x19
front brake dia	7[14]	7[14]	8	8	8	8
rear brake dia	7	7	7	7	7	7
wheelbase in.	56[15]	55.5	55	55.5	56	55.5

[1] - 1956-7.8,1960-8.1,1961-8.25
[2] - 1962-9.5
[3] - 1960-7.6,1961-8.25
[4] - 1958-coil
[5] - 1962-mag
[6] - 1958-alt
[7] - 1955-376
[8] - 1956-4.75,1960-5.00
[9] - 1964-5.28
[10] - 1960-4.75
[11] - 1960-3.6
[12] - 1953-3.25x19
[13] - 1953-3.00x19
[14] - 1954-8
[15] - 1953-54.5

Dominator Specifications

Model	99 Nomad	99SS	650	650SS	Mercury	Atlas
years	1958-60	1961-62	1961-63	1962-68	1969-70	1962-68
bore mm	68	68	68	68	68	73
stroke mm	82	82	89	89	89	89
capacity cc	596	596	646	646	646	745
comp. ratio	9.0	8.25	8.3[1]	8.9	8.9	7.6
ignition	mag	coil	mag[2]	mag[3]	cap	mag[3]
generator	alt	alt	alt	alt	alt	alt
carb type	276 (2)	376 (2)	389 (2)[4]	376 (2)[5]	930	376[6]
carb size	1-1/16	1-1/16	1-1/8	1-1/16[7]	30 mm	1-1/16[7]
top gear	5.00	4.75	4.53	4.53	4.53	4.53
petrol - gall	2.25	3.6	3.6	3.6	3.6	3.6
front tyre	3.00x21	3.00x19	3.00x19	3.00x19	3.00x19	3.00x19
rear tyre	4.00x19	3.50x19	3.50x19	3.50x19	3.50x19	3.50x19
front brake dia	8	8	8	8	8	8
rear brake dia	7	7	7	7	7	7
wheelbase in.	55	55.5	55.5	55.5	55.5	55.5

[1] - 1962-8.9
[2] - 1962-coil
[3] - 1968-cap
[4] - 1962-single 389
[5] - 1967-930
[6] - 1964-twin 376,1967 twin 930
[7] - 1967-30 mm

Dominator Specifications

Model	Atlas MX	N15CS'N'	N15CS	P11	P11A	Ranger
years	1963-64	1964-67	1968	1967	1968	1968
bore mm	73	73	73	73	73	73
stroke mm	89	89	89	89	89	89
capacity cc	745	745	745	745	745	745
comp. ratio	7.6	7.6	7.6	7.6	7.6	7.6
ignition	mag	mag	cap	cap	cap	cap
generator	alt	alt	alt	alt	alt	alt
carb type	389 (2)	389 (2)[1]	930 (2)	930 (2)	930 (2)	930 (2)
carb size	1-1/8	1-1/8[2]	30 mm	30 mm	30 mm	30 mm
top gear	5.00	5.00	5.00	4.53	4.53	4.53
petrol - gall	2.0	2.0	2.0	2.25	2.25	2.25
front tyre	3.50x19	3.50x19	3.50x19	3.25x19	3.25x19	3.25x19
rear tyre	4.00x18	4.00x18	4.00x18	4.00x18	4.00x18	4.00x18
front brake dia	8	8	8	7	7	7
rear brake dia	7	7	7	7	7	7
wheelbase in.	55.4	55.4	55.4	56.9	56.9	56.9

[1] - 1967-930

[2] - 1967-30 mm